# J-LO'S MISSION

By

## Margaret Brazear

Copyright © Margaret Brazear 2017

*J-Lo's mission is to prevent other Cavalier King Charles Spaniels from suffering as she has*

# DEDICATION

THIS BOOK IS DEDICATED TO J-LO, A SPECIAL LITTLE
MIRACLE DOG WHO GAVE A MAN BACK HIS LIFE.

# TABLE OF CONTENTS

# THE STORY OF J-LO

J-Lo is a pretty little Ruby coloured Cavalier King Charles Spaniel girl who was born on 15th August 2009. She is a little miracle dog and this is her story.

Post traumatic stress had kept Patrick locked inside his own house for many months, sinking deeper into a black depression, and J-Lo was, literally, the little person who saved his life.

Patrick's experiences, which will not be described here, had made him wary and there were very few people he felt able to trust.

He had never had a dog, or a pet of any kind, and when a social worker suggested he get a dog, if only to get him out of the house and into the fresh air, he was not at all keen on the idea. After all, a dog is a huge responsibility and Patrick thought he had enough on his shoulders without taking on the welfare of a living creature who would depend on him completely.

But the more he thought about it, the more he realised that a dog was one creature he could trust and the notion of sharing his life with a little furry person became more appealing.

He had no idea what sort of dog he wanted, but he searched the internet and finally settled on a Cavalier King Charles Spaniel. The breed was ideal for Patrick's purposes, bred to be just what he was looking for - a friend and companion.

This was not only a dog who would get him out of the house and meeting people, she was someone he could talk to. Nobody who doesn't love dogs would understand that sensible conversation can be had with a canine and if you watch closely, they will talk back. This was but one of the joys Patrick was destined to learn.

He found a breeder many miles away, but it seemed worth the journey to find the right puppy.

Patrick and his friend, Steve, drove to Birmingham to see the litter. It was a normal, family home and they met both parents and six adorable little puppies. There were five little boys, but just one little lady and, although she was the runt of the litter, it was love at first sight.

At the time she cost £900 and she slept on Patrick's lap all the way home. Then she was only the size of his hand, a tiny, helpless little bundle of fur who was going to give her new owner back his life.

An accident almost happened on the way home, when Steve swerved to avoid a man walking along the middle of the slip road in the dark. The man threw one of his trainers at the car and cursed them. Perhaps that was an omen; who knows?

J-Lo's mission seemed to be working, as Patrick was now forced to leave the house to show his new little friend what fun was to be had outside. He also found that out there were other dog owners who were always willing to discuss their own canines and talk to Patrick about his.

Training progressed well enough and for the first nine months of her life, J-Lo seemed to be a fine, happy and healthy little dog.

The first symptom of her later illness came when she began to scratch frantically at her ears and she would shake for no apparent reason.

The scratching of the ears can mean many things in a canine, especially those long eared breeds. Often it is nothing more than ear mites or even an ear infection, but it should always be investigated. Even these minor ailments cause the animal discomfort and pain; they must be treated.

The tremors, however, are something else again.

All this was terrifying to J-Lo's devoted owner and he immediately took her to the local veterinary surgeon, who told him that they believed she had some neurological problems.

Patrick immediately agreed to a brain scan and J-Lo was referred to the Animal Health Trust to carry out this process.

J-Lo was diagnosed with Syringomyelia (SM), a condition where the skull is too small for the brain, causing serious pain for the dog with the potential for paralysis of the back legs, stiffness of the neck and fits of spasm and pain.

How helpless could the owner of a dog with this awful disease feel? To see the love of his life suffering so and not being able to reach into that skull and pluck out the pain, take it into himself. If only he could. And how angry he must have felt, must still feel, to know that dogs are still being bred without the proper tests for this incapacitating illness?

On medical advice, Patrick informed the breeder of the diagnosis, but they refused to believe it and would not commit to discontinue breeding from the same parents. There is nothing that can be done to stop more puppies being condemned to suffer as J-Lo has suffered. This needs to change; breeders who are in denial like this should be prosecuted.

J-Lo was prescribed a mixture of two drugs, Gabapentin and Metacam, designed to relieve the symptoms of SM. For about a year they were successful and J-Lo lived a full and active life. She always enjoyed her long walks and loved meeting other dogs on the different excursions.

It is in the Cavalier's nature to be both people and dog friendly and J-Lo was no exception. Patrick was delighted, thinking that, as long as she had her medicine, all would be well.

As time went on, it seemed clear that the SM had taken hold yet again. The tremors returned, sometimes she screamed out in pain and after another visit to the Animal Health Trust she was prescribed Onsia as well. The scratching also returned and she began to have fits. She could not stand even to be stroked on her head.

The combination of drugs kept the SM under control until J-Lo was nearly five. She needed regular brain scans, every six months, to make sure that the condition was under control, but Patrick and the Animal Health Trust were content that all seemed well.

But Patrick was not allowed to relax, to look forward to a worry-free life with a healthy little dog. Her SM began to really spiral out of control and her fits got worse. She began to pant a lot and was bought an air conditioning machine to help with this problem. But it did little good. More and more screaming fits ensued as well as shaking, paralysis of her back legs, which thank God was temporary, and more and more visits to the Animal Health Trust.

There followed a year or more of stress, late night visits to the vets, overnight stays and juggling all the different drugs. But it seemed that miracles do happen and after more tests and scans at the Animal Health Trust, no sign of SM remained. She had been cured of this terrible disease, actually cured!

Can you imagine the relief, the absolute joy? She was cured! She could live a normal, happy life, like any other dog. At last she could start to be a proper dog.

But Patrick's joy was short lived. Still not well, strange lumps began to appear on J-Lo's back. They could be felt through her fur and of course, Patrick immediately thought *Cancer!* But this new problem did not stop there; she also developed breathing problems.

All Cavaliers have been bred over the years with shorter noses, probably because it looked cute, and this has resulted in snoring, which was considered normal.

A local veterinary surgeon who had been looking after J-Lo became very attached to her and, having a young family, often took her home. This was in part to keep an eye on her and in part so that Patrick could get a night's uninterrupted sleep. The snoring was so loud, it was difficult to have a conversation in the same room, but there were other problems that went unnoticed. J-Lo would fall asleep very suddenly and often fell off the bed or chair in her sleep.

The local vet returned J-Lo after having her for a weekend and remarked that the snoring was nothing to worry about. But Patrick knew his little dog and decided to take some videos, just to have a record and perhaps show them to the Animal Health Trust on the next visit.

As fate would have it, J-Lo's regular vet was unavailable when Patrick next visited so the videos were shown to the senior vet, who was instantly alarmed. She informed Patrick that the symptoms were typical of major respiratory problems. The Animal Health Trust agreed to see him immediately, but Patrick was distraught that the condition had gone unnoticed.

The problem was diagnosed as an excess of fatty deposits in the neck. They decided to operate with the obvious dangers of giving an already unhealthy and slightly overweight dog an anaesthetic. Still, it had to be done, and she was there for six weeks, during which time she had the operation and was closely monitored during her recovery.

You can imagine that the reunion between dog and human was a wonderful thing to see. Although Patrick had been to visit quite regularly, he was over the moon to get J-Lo back home.

While they had her under anaesthetic, the surgeon decided they might as well remove some of the lumps on her back to investigate. The lumps were benign tumours, thank heavens, which was a relief but her troubles did not end there.

She needed to go on a serious diet to lose three stone, as the extra weight was doing her heart no good at all. Neither was it helping her legs.

It should be noted that her first severe symptoms appeared after J-Lo suffered a cough. The cough caused pressure on her skull and pushed some brain matter through and into her spine, which caused terrible pain.

Although benign, the lumps progressed to J-Lo's eardrums but their removal caused deafness. She also suffered from facial nerve paralysis which has prevented her from blinking and led to a condition known as dry eye. Patrick has had to apply eye drops three times a day and the miracle is that his perseverance has paid off. From total dry eyes, J-Lo can now blink again and even has some tears.

A new miracle occurred just a little while ago. From being completely deaf, she started to react to noises and hearing tests proved that her hearing has returned. Not 100%, but enough to function and know when there is someone at the door.

J-Lo is now on more medications as she has been found to have a heart murmur, a urinary tract infection and a tumour in her bladder which reduces the size of the bladder and makes her urinate a lot, and she now has Cushings disease. This last is more of a problem than it might be as, while trying to keep her weight down, the disease makes her very, very hungry.

Despite all these problems, all this trauma and all these illnesses, that little tail just keeps on wagging!

J-Lo was chosen by Patrick to help him over a serious issue. All he expected at the time was that the little dog would get him out of the house, force him to greet the world. Instead, she has totally consumed his thoughts until his own problems no longer matter.

She has done her job and never was a dog better loved.

This Christmas J-Lo is still bringing joy to Patrick and everyone else who knows her. And she is still smiling.

She would love to be completely healthy and she would love to wish you all a happy christmas.

*December 2017*

J-Lo, a seven year old Cavalier King Charles Spaniel, suffers from several different health problems, including severe sleep apnoea, syringomyelia and facial nerve paralysis, which causes her problems with her eyes. J-Lo's sleep apnoea means she often wakes up suddenly because she can't breathe. This is clearly very distressing for both J-Lo and her very devoted owner, Patrick, and also means that J-Lo isn't sleeping properly and is tired all the time.

J-Lo has been referred to the Animal Health Trust (AHT), near Newmarket, several times and has used almost the full range of the AHT's state-of-the-art equipment, including MRI and CT scans, fluoroscopy and endoscopy to help the vets of many different specialties at the AHT investigate her different health problems. She's a fantastic example of how the different specialist vets, including medical physicians, surgeons, neurologists, dermatologists, ophthalmologists, radiologists and anaesthetists, along with the fantastic nursing team at the AHT, work closely together to ensure the best possible care for the patients.

James Warland, one of the vets who is treating J-Lo at the AHT, said: "J-Lo's sleep apnoea has got so extreme that she has had to be hospitalised for monitoring and more tests to work out the best way to treat her. She has had surgery in the past, but as she is currently overweight we have been using hydrotherapy and a weight loss programme to improve her overall weight, health and fitness, and hope to be able to avoid more surgery.

"The main problem with J-Lo's eyes is that the facial nerve paralysis prevents her from blinking. She has had a temporary surgery on her eyelids to help protect her eyes while we hope the nerve function will slowly return. Fortunately most dogs cope very well with such nerve paralysis, which can be permanent, as long as we can keep their eyes healthy. We're very pleased Patrick and J-Lo are helping to raise funds for the AHT, as every penny of profit the AHT makes treating animals is re-invested into research to improve the health and wellbeing of animals. We look forward to seeing J-Lo for a check-up again soon."

# HEALTH TESTS

Anyone thinking of buying a Cavalier King Charles Spaniel should ask themselves what they hope for in their new dog. Is he/she going to be a show dog or a companion and pet. How important to the dog's future is the breed standard?

Whatever you decide, do not be fooled into believing that health tests don't matter if the dog is going to be just a pet.

Believe it or not, this is an excuse many poor breeders will give unsuspecting buyers to explain a lack of health tests. They are important in any dog and in the Cavalier, there are many potential health issues a prospective owner should consider.

The first and most important is Syringomyelia (SM). Be sure your new puppy's parents have been tested for this horrible illness, as it is hereditary. Basically, it is caused by the dog's skull being too small to accommodate the mass of its brain.

Breed standards which state a small skull as essential in the breed are the major cause of this complaint, as breeders wanting to do well at top dog shows have for years been breeding for a smaller skull. This is the result and J-Lo's story will tell you how heartbreaking it is for the owner and painful and debilitating for the dog.

Tests should also be carried out for heart murmurs and eye problems. The following are the health tests advised by the UK Kennel Club:

Eye disease - multifocal retinal dysplasia (littler screening); hereditary cataract (annual testing); multiple ocular defects (litter screening).

Hip dysplasia. The breed average is 21 so healthy parents should be lower than this

Chiari malformation syringomyelia - occipital bone

malformation which squashes the hindbrain, blocks the normal flow of cerebrospinal fluid and causes pockets of fluid within the spinal cord). This causes pain and other neurological symptoms. An extremely high incidence in this breed.

Most Cavaliers have the malformation and 70% will develop SM. Potential owners should go to a breeder who uses the BVA/KC CMSM scheme of testing rather than any other scheme.

Any dog with the large eyes, like the Cavalier, should have tests for eye problems as these are the dogs most in danger of being affected. That does not rule out eye problems in other breeds, not at all. Indeed, the Akita, a very large dog, is well known for having a tendency to suffer from ingrowing eyelashes, which scratch the eyeball and cause blindness and terrible pain.

No doglover wants to see his/her dog go through unnecessary pain, when a few simple tests would prevent it.

What did surprise me was the need for hip scoring in such a small dog. I always equate hip dysplasia with large dogs, especially giants, but it seems the little Cavalier also has a tendency to the deformity.

The expected lifespan of the Cavalier King Charles spaniel is between 9 and 15 years.

All these tests are the reason a good pedigree dog is so expensive to buy as a puppy, and it is well worth the extra money. Again, many unscrupulous breeders count on people wanting to pay less, so they skimp on tests. It will be a lot more expensive in the long run. Patrick will confirm that, as J-Lo's veterinary expenses have reached almost £100,000 and still rising.

The insurance will not cover all of it and all profits from this book will go towards paying them.

# KENNEL COUGH

Kennel cough is a common disease which is caused by close proximity to dogs who are, or who have been infected.

It is extremely common in the summer months, when dogs go into kennels whilst their owners are away on holiday. Because of all the dogs together, there is invariably an outbreak of this disease.

Symptoms include harsh, dry coughing, tiredness and loss of appetite. Occasionally the illness can progress to pneumonia.

Treatment may include cough suppressants to alleviate the symptoms and antibacterials to relieve the disease, though these will not eliminate the infection.

It is not uncommon for a dog to contract kennel cough at sometime in his life, and although it is rarely fatal, infectiousness can last for several weeks after recovery.

If you suspect that your dog has

contracted the disease, immediate veterinary treatment is essential to alleviate suffering. You need to tell everyone whose dogs he has been in contact with. You must also keep him away from other animals for some weeks afterwards.

The disease can spread to other animals, including cats and horses.

There is now a nasal vaccination against this horrible disease, which involves drops into the nostrils, rather than an injection. This vaccination can be given to a dog of any age and it is safe for puppies as young as three weeks.

Ensure that your puppy has these drops to keep him safe from this nasty disease.

# CANINE RABIES

Canine Rabies has been eliminated in the United Kingdom. No cases of the disease have been found in the UK since 1902 and the last reported case from animals being brought into the country was in 1946.

The very word "rabies" fills one with fear. Because I live in the UK, I have never seen a real live case of this disease, but I do know that it will turn a normally placid and gentle dog into a killer.

Most countries, though, still have to be careful of their dogs catching the disease, which is almost always fatal and can be spread between dogs and other species, including humans.

The disease is spread by the bite or saliva of an infected animal. Early symptoms include irritation of the affected area, fever, change in behaviour and dilated pupils. However symptoms will not begin to show for at least four weeks after infection. The second phase of the infection causes aggression, disorientation and sensivity to light.

The final phase is paralysis, respiratory failure, hydrophobia (fear of water) and death.

Rabies is a killer, both of animals and humans. Any mammal can contract the disease, but it is normally carried by wild animals such as bats, racoons and wolves.

If you do not live in one of the countries which have eliminated this disease, be sure that your puppy is vaccinated.

# COLOURS

As with any KC registered pedigree dog, the Cavalier comes in acceptable colours and there is a great variety with these little darlings.

The Ruby - J-Lo's colour
For showing, white markings are undesirable.

The Black and Tan

The Black and Tan should be Raven black with tan markings above the eyes, on cheeks, inside ears, on chest and legs and underside of tail. The official version is that white markings are undesirable, but this puppy was so cute, I couldn't resist!

## The Blenheim

The Blenheim should have rich chestnut markings, well broken up, on pearly white background. Markings should be evenly divided on the head, leaving room between the ears for lozenge mark or spot.

Tricolour

The Tricolour is black and white, well spaced, broken up, with tan markings over eyes, cheeks, inside ears and inside legs. Also on underside of tail.

All these stipulated markings and colours are required by the Kennel Club and are very important if you want to show your dog. If you don't, then the exact colours hardly matter except for the question of unscrupulous breeders.

It is a fact that these breeders will try to fool inexperienced puppy buyers into believing that any other colour is rare and therefore more valuable. I have seen dogs advertised at twice the accepted price because of their 'rare' colouring. In actual fact, these colours are not accepted by the Kennel Club and should be selling for less money, not more.

# BREED STANDARD

Should you want to show your Cavalier, you will need to know the Kennel Club standard for the breed. Apart from the colours, already stated, there are other requirements for a show dog.

Your dog will need to be active, graceful and well balanced. It also states a gentle expression, but all friendly dogs will have one of those.

Your dog will need to be sporting, affectionate and fearless. That last is a little vague, in my opinion. The fearlessness or otherwise of any dog depends on its breeding and upbringing.

Your dog's head and skull should be almost flat between the ears. It is this insistence on a small, flat skull that has caused so many incidences of syringomyelia. The Kennel Club are now stating that this is almost a thing of the past, but it still needs careful consideration.

Any ethical breeder will have stopped breeding any dogs with this disease, but not all are ethical. Many are interested only in money and nothing else and do not want to discard their breeding stock, in whom they have a vast financial interest.

Nostrils should be black and well developed without flesh marks, muzzle tapered. Lips should be well developed but not pendulous. The face well filled below eyes.

The eyes should be large, dark and round but not prominent. They should be spaced well apart.

The ears should be long and set high with lots of feather.

The mouth should have strong jaws with a regular scissor bite, i.e. upper teeth closely overlapping lower teeth and set square of the jaws.

Your dog should have a moderate length, slightly arched neck.

The body should be short and have a good spring, level back.

The feet should be compact, cushioned and well feathered.

Your dog's tail should be in balance with the body, well set and carried happily but never much above the level of the back. The Cavalier doesn't usually hold his tail up when he is secure, like a lot of other dogs. Many breeds will hold their tail straight and the Cavalier is no exception.

In the past, the tail has been docked but no more than a third should be removed. It is now illegal in the United Kingdom to dock tails or ears, unless the dog is a working dog.

He should have a free moving gait and be elegant in action.

Your dog's coat should be long and silky and free from curl.

Weight needs to be carefully monitored in both show and pet dogs. An overweight dog will have other health problems that could affect the dog's heart and joints. The Cavalier should weigh between 12 and 18 lbs.

# CAVALIER HISTORY

There are two breeds, the King Charles Spaniel and the Cavalier King Charles Spaniel. Until 1945, the two breeds were shown together, but the popularity of the Cavalier increased to the point where few of the original King Charles Spaniels are seen today.

The King Charles Spaniel

When my son was at school, his headmistress had one of these originals (see above) and she would bring him into school every day. The children loved him and he loved them. She was never seen without her little dog.

It was this original little toy spaniel that is seen in many pictures of King Charles II, after whom the breed was named. He would rarely be seen without three or four of them following behind.

Unfortunately, back then in the seventeenth century, nobody thought of housetraining a dog and these little spaniels would relieve themselves all over the palace.

Imagine that with all those long skirts sweeping across the floor!

It wasn't until the time of Queen Victoria that showing became popular and serious breeding began to emerge, with standards and exact colours and measurements. This produced the larger Cavalier King Charles Spaniel that we see today.

Both breeds of dogs have always been companion dogs. They are derived from the working spaniels, but have never had a job of work of their own except the most important job of being a friend to their owners.

# GROOMING

Grooming the Cavalier is easy enough, but their fur is silky and grows quite long. This means it can get tangled easily. Imagine your own hair if you don't brush it for days! Being a small dog, she is easy to pick up and put on a table and hold still for grooming, but like any dog, she needs to be introduced to grooming from the earliest possible age.

In a pet dog, it is easier and more comfortable in the summer months to clip the fur. This is usual with a pet spaniel of any variety but for showing, no clipping is allowed.

The dog will need daily brushing with a medium strength bristle brush to keep the oils evenly flowing. It is a water resistant coat which will need shampooing twice to remove all the dirt.

No dog should be bathed too often as that destroys the oils which protect the dog's skin.

Drying should be first done by a rub down with a towel and should be followed by a dog hairdryer, or blaster. This can also be useful for removing loose hair on a dry coat.

The feet on the Cavalier should be left long and fluffy.

# HOUSE TRAINING

When you house train a puppy, or even a full grown dog, the first thing to learn is the way that dogs think. They learn by association. It is no use yelling at him after he has gone in the wrong place - it is too late by then and he will associate your presence with being scolded. He has no idea what he is supposed to have done and showing him will not improve that situation.

All he will know is that you come home and he gets shouted at. So, do you want your Cavalier to come and greet you with his tail wagging? Or do you want him to run away and hide as soon as he hears you coming?

It is also important to realise that you cannot house train a dog if you are not there. Believe it or not, I have heard of people who never taught their dog to go outside or to ask to go outside, because they truly believed the dog would just know. A cat is a different creature; give the cat a dirt tray and she will use it because their instinct is to bury their waste.

The same cannot be said of dogs and I'm sure you don't want your house to smell like King Charles' palace!

You need to watch your dog carefully, look for signs that he is sniffing around, looking for a place to go. As soon as you see this, you must pick him up and take him outside into the garden. Do not just leave him out there - he will forget about going and want to follow you inside. You need to stay with him, wait for him to go no matter how long it takes. You can associate a word with this, as soon as he performs, but not until.

Always have a pocket of treats so that as soon as he goes, you can tell him what a good boy (or girl) he is and give him a treat.

You should also take him outside after he has eaten and when he wakes up. Puppies will toilet a lot. It is hard work keeping up with them, but it will not take long provided that you pay attention to every little move he makes.

Once he has toileted where he is supposed to give him lots and lots of praise and treats, then let him back inside.

What if he starts to go in the house? You simply pick him up and take him outside, even if it is too late, and say nothing. He will not understand if you scold him for going in the house; he will think he is being scolded for doing what he must do. The result of this will be that he will either find somewhere to go where you cannot see him, or he will wait until you are out of the room.

In his mind, he gets scolded if you are there; he does not get scolded if you are not there, and you will have forfeited your chance to praise him for going in the right place. No way is he going to perform with you hanging about!

If he does toilet in the house, and it will happen on occasion, be sure to clean it thoroughly with a biological washing powder or one of the many products available from pet stores. If the smell still lingers, he is more likely to go in that same spot again.

It is a good idea to remove rugs and cover carpet with heavy plastic sheeting. This is easier to clean and will ensure that the smell does not linger.

The same principles apply with a full grown dog who has never been housetrained, perhaps living outside in kennels.

I have managed to housetrain a puppy in just a few days using these methods and even a full grown dog in less than a week. But you must keep calm; if you are stressed about it, the dog will never get the message.

# POSITIVE TRAINING

Dog training has come a long way in the past sixty years or so, so if you think you need to be your dog's pack leader, you need to rethink your own position and that of your dog. Unfortunately, some trainers still cling to this myth, at the expense of dogs and their welfare.

Back in the 1920's, a study was carried out using a group of unrelated, captive wolves. These brilliant researchers came up with the theory that there was an Alpha Male among the wolves, a leader to whom the others deferred.

They noticed that this "alpha" wolf always ate first and that he positioned himself higher than the others. This is where the daft idea of not allowing your dog on the sofa or bed came from - he mustn't be allowed to be higher than you. I even read once on a forum a man looking for advice because his 'knowledgeable' wife was afraid to sit down near her new, full grown Great Dane because if she sat he was higher than her! Unbelievable rubbish.

Whilst it would be difficult to place a Cavalier higher than its human, the principal still applies. The only reason to keep your dog off the furniture is because you don't want hairs and dirt on your furniture.

Since that time, it has been established that wolves do not live in packs which have a leader; they live in family units where the leaders are the parent couple. Once the cubs have grown they will go off and establish their own family unit, but in the meantime, when food is scarce, it is the babies who eat first, never the parents.

Unfortunately, despite much research to the contrary, this theory has embedded itself into our culture and we still have many so-called trainers spouting this nonsense about having to be your dog's pack leader, having to dominate him

This theory has not only been discredited, but the original researcher who came up with it has stated many, many times that he was wrong!

The first thing to remember is that dogs are not wolves anyway. They are thousands of years evolved from being wolves, they do not behave like wolves, they do not live in family units, and in the wild they will fight over resources such as food, shelter and females, never will they fight to establish their leadership.

This in turn means that whilst one dog might win the much sought after food, another might win the female. There is no defined leader.

How many times have you read or seen on TV that the dog will think of you as part of his pack, and that you have to establish yourself as his pack leader? To do this you are supposed to go through doors first (how many doors does a wild dog need to open?) You need to always eat first (the dog isn't even noticing). You must not let him on the sofa! Well, how is he going to get on my lap and have a cuddle if he is not allowed on the sofa?

You may also have read or seen that

your dog is trying to dominate you, that he is trying to dominate the door (no, he is just excited about visitors), he is trying to dominate you by squashing you up into the corner (no he is just after your cup of tea).

One of the silliest things I ever read was that if my dog puts both paws on my lap, he is being dominant! I would say he either wants a cuddle or he is trying to tell me something.

Dogs do not want to dominate humans.

The most damaging conclusion that came out of this original study is that the pack leader will pin another dog down, performing an "alpha roll" to let the other dog know who is boss. Pinning a dog down in this way will only intimidate and scare him into biting, as he sees this as his only defence.

They failed completely to notice that the dog positioned himself on his side or his back, as a sign of submission. This is something that a lot of dogs do as though he is saying "I don't want a fight, you win". No other dog is pinning him in this position and the idea of pinning your dog down to make him behave is extremely damaging, both mentally and emotionally.

Positive dog training is no different from the way people have been training wild animals for years. You would not put a shock collar on a whale, would you? Captive creatures like that will not perform tricks because some human threatens them - they will do it for rewards.

Dogs have a language all their own and it is subtle, easy for us mere humans to miss.

There are books that have been written by highly qualified experts, and they will help you to understand what your dog is actually saying. If you get his body language wrong, you will do yourself and your dog a lot of harm. Many highly qualified animal behaviourists have been studying canine behaviour for many years and they are all agreed on one thing – dogs are not pack animals. They are social creatures who want nothing more than to be close to their humans and give them companionship. You will establish yourself as leader simply by being the one with the resources.

So, do Cavalier dogs need special training? No. All dogs deserve to be trained using love, praise and rewards.

So what is positive dog training? It is the simple skill of giving something in return for something.

You need to build a relationship with your Cavalier so that he will do anything to please you. None of this is difficult, but it does take time and patience, especially if he has had no training. If you adopt a dog from a shelter, it is likely that you will have to start from scratch.

The secret is to realise that your dog is an intelligent creature. All dogs have different breed traits, depending on what they were originally bred for, and Cavaliers are no exception. But they were bred to be pets and are naturally friendly. You can destroy that amicable nature if you don't respect his intellect.

If he likes treats, give him a treat when he does what you want. When you call him back, give him a treat when he comes to you, no matter how long it takes. If he knows he'll get a reward he is more likely to do what you want.

Teach him to sit by holding a treat over his mouth and gradually guiding it backwards until his head goes up. He will sit because he cannot put his head up and stay standing and when he does sit, as soon as his bottom hits the ground, that is the time to say sit. That way he associates the action with the word.

The same goes for every action.

I have had dogs for more than forty years and have trained them all myself. It is not difficult, but it does take patience.

I often hear people saying they have tried everything. That is usually their problem. It's no good starting a method and changing when it doesn't work straight away. You need to keep going until it does work, otherwise you only achieve a very confused dog.

# BREEDERS

Finding good Cavalier King Charles spaniel breeders is essential if you are thinking about a puppy.

As Cavaliers become one of the most popular dog breeds, they are being bred more and more by puppy farmers and back yard breeders.

Just to be clear: A puppy farmer (or puppy mill) is one who will keep many different breeds of dog, usually in appalling conditions. These dogs will be kept outside in kennels with the bare minimum of comfort provided.

Their bitches are overbred. They no sooner have a litter and they are being mated once more to provide more puppies to sell to make more money. That is the prime consideration of a puppy farmer - money.

Their puppies will not be registered with kennel clubs. The UK Kennel Club states a maximum of four litters per bitch. The American and other nation's clubs might have different rules.

Puppy farmers' dogs will not be vaccinated, so all sorts of horrible diseases can be passed on to the puppies.

The puppies will have had no health checks, no worming, no anything really and are very often sold off at 6 weeks or younger, which is a prime socialisation time for the puppy to learn from his littermates.

There will definitely be no health certificates. The parents' hipscores will not be taken before breeding, so your puppy could well end up suffering from hip dysplasia. No eye tests or heart scans will have been taken either.

Back yard breeders can be much the same, only on a smaller scale.

Sometimes an owner will breed one litter from her bitch. There is an old wives' tale that it is good for a bitch to have one litter before being spayed, which is quite frankly, rubbish.

These people mean well, and could have very healthy puppies, but they should have those health tests done before breeding. It is vitally important in any dog, but in a Cavalier it is even more important. With the number of potential health problems in the breed, it is essential to avoid these parasites.

None of the above are good Cavalier breeders

# HOW TO AVOID PUPPY FARMERS

Puppy farmers are easy enough to spot, if you do your homework.

Never take a puppy that is under eight weeks of age.

Never arrange to collect a puppy from a neutral location - the breeder does not want you to see their premises.

Make sure you see all the puppies, in the house with their mother.

Make sure you have their health certificates, their full pedigrees and their kennel club registration.

Never buy from a pet store, no matter how reputable. They get their stocks from puppy farmers.

If the breeder does not want you to visit before you collect your puppy, alarm bells should ring.

Although many puppy farmers try to charge the same price as a good, health tested, puppy, be very suspicious if the puppy is a lot less than it should be.

Good Cavalier breeders will want to meet you, will ask about your experience and circumstances, they will want to know how you are with their dogs.

# HOW TO FIND A GOOD BREEDER

A good breeder will breed their dogs to preserve and improve the breed. Although they have to cover their expenses, and health tests are very expensive, they are more interested in the puppy's welfare than they are in the money.

The first place to start is the breed club. There are Cavalier breed clubs all over the world, and they will always advise you as to what you are taking on, and provide you with the name of a good breeder. They have nothing to gain by this freely given information, except to contribute to the welfare of the dogs.

If you live in the United Kingdom, a well respected site for finding a reputable breeder is Champdogs. On the Champdogs site you can view your puppy's pedigree. Look for ancestors typed in red - these are champion dogs.

You may have to go on a waiting list for a puppy. Breeders of this calibre do not breed all the time and they usually have a waiting list for their puppies. Try not to be impatient, it will be the best thing in the long run. A really good puppy is worth waiting for.

You have decided on a Cavalier puppy, you are excited, can't wait, and you want him now! Trust me, it is not worth it. You may be lucky enough to find a good breeder who has a puppy left; it happens. Sometimes their buyer changes their mind, circumstances change, but if that does not happen, do not rush into the next best thing. You will end up regretting it.

You can usually get a list of approved breeders from the Kennel Club. Go through the list, starting with the nearest. If they don't have a puppy available or expected, they will know someone who does.

Never buy from a breeder who is breeding several breeds. If someone is advertising, it is likely they are not a reputable breeder, but it is not certain.

As an example, eight years ago my seventeen year old granddaughter wanted a cocker spaniel puppy for Christmas. Knowing that most breeders won't part with a pup before Christmas, I didn't think we'd find one and I was reluctant when we went to see an advertised little of eleven pups.

The owners also owned both the mother and father and this was a one off littler. I was dubious, but this little black cocker, aptly named Rascal, has been a wonderful addition to our family.

It can work, but please don't believe everything you are told, particularly if you are inexperienced at dog ownership.

# CHOOSING A PUPPY

Choosing a puppy is not something to be done impulsively. A lot of consideration must be given to this choice, do not let your heart rule your head.

You should be able to see the litter of puppies in the breeder's house, with their mother.

What is their mother like? Is she a friendly dog? Does she come to say hello, does she seem pleased to show off her puppies?

A good breeder will breed for temperament as well as health, so be sure that the mother is an approachable dog. Do not be fooled by being told that she is defensive of her pups - this is rarely the case.

The puppies should come to you willingly, not appear nervous but should be curious about you.

If the breeder has young children in the house, watch for signs that the children have been allowed to pull the puppies around at will. This sort of treatment can result in a permanently nervous and sometimes aggressive dog.

You also need to see the puppy's pedigree and make sure no interbreeding has been going on.

Look carefully at the mother when choosing a puppy and preferably the father as well. Do they look like a Cavalier is supposed to look like? Or do they look more like you wouldn't really know what breed they are?

A good breeder will not allow a puppy to leave its litter until it is at least eight weeks old, sometimes ten weeks. This is because a puppy needs to be with his littermates where he will learn bite inhibition and other dog language which you will find it difficult to teach.

A responsible breeder will not sell a puppy just before Christmas unless they know you very well or have special references for you. They are always wary of people trying to buy a puppy as a Christmas present for someone who may not be prepared to have a dog, and may not really want one. People seem to think a puppy would be a good present for their little nephew or niece, may have heard someone in the family say that they like Cavaliers. That doesn't mean that they really want one or would know how to care for one. Good breeders are extremely careful about this sort of thing.

Christmas puppies also suffer from the time of year, the excitement, the noise. A puppy must be kept quiet for his first few days in his new home and Christmas is not the time to do this.

Would you believe that I once read a forum post by a breeder of Red Setters who said that someone had wanted to have one of her puppies, just for over Christmas, because he was red and would look nice in the photographs! This is the sort of mentality breeders have to deal with, so do not be offended if your chosen breeder will not allow any of their puppies to go just before Christmas.

A good breeder will also ask you lots of questions. They will want to know if you have experience of dogs, how much experience, what sort of house you have, are you at work all day?

Do not be offended by these questions - they are a sign of a caring breeder.

They may be reluctant to sell a puppy to a first time dog owner and they may refuse to sell to someone who is at work all day.

A good breeder will also tell you that if, for any reason, you cannot keep the dog, they will take him or her back, no matter what age he is.

They will want to meet you and have you see the puppies when they are about four weeks old. This is for your benefit as well as theirs, as you can assess the situation and get to know the breeder while they get to know you. It is well worth doing, even if you have to travel a long way to do it. But do not be surprised if there is a waiting list and you have to wait for the next litter.

# THINGS TO BEWARE OF

Do not find your puppy in the free ads or on internet sites. Be very suspicious if the puppies are not kept in the house in a proper birthing pen. They should not be outside in a kennel. No good breeder would keep their puppies that way.

Never buy a puppy from a pet store, no matter how reputable. They get their stocks from puppy farmers.

Be very suspicious if the price is too low. Prices change all the time, but look on a good site like Champdogs to get an idea of how much you should be paying.

You may think you are getting a bargain. You are not. You will end up paying a lot more in vet bills and heartache in the long run.

Unfortunately, it is human nature to feel they have got a bargain. I have lost count of the number of people who have told me, very smugly, that they have seen puppies much cheaper than I paid for mine. They seem to think that I will feel that I have been conned, but I know better.

And it is just this attitude which keeps the puppy farmers and back yard breeders in business.

There is no such thing as a bargain when it comes to buying a puppy and if you are thinking mostly about the price, then perhaps it is not the right time to have a puppy.

Of course, some puppy farmers and backyard breeders try to sell their unhealth tested puppies at top pedigree prices, so all things need to be considered.

Run away, very fast, if the breeder wants to meet you in a neutral location to hand over a puppy. That is always a sign of a puppy farmer who does not want anyone to see their premises.

Try to find out all you can on the phone. Once you have seen these cute little fluffy puppies, it is very often the hardest thing in the world to walk away if things don't feel right.

I heard a tale once about some

inexperienced people who answered an advertisement for a Rottweiler puppy. They were asked to meet with the breeder at a service station to hand over the pup and pay; they were asked to meet in the evening, after dark. The breeder arrived with a black holdall, the zipper of which he opened just enough to see the black and tan fur of the tiny pup, but he didn't want to disturb him as he was sleeping.

It wasn't until the people arrived home with their Rottweiler puppy that they discovered they had bought a guinea pig. Yes, really.

Then there was the celebrity who complained on a talk show that her very expensive and rare dog would not touch dog food. In fact she was at her wit's end and had even tried feeding it human food, but the dog wasn't interested in that either.

On producing a photograph of the very expensive, rare breed of dog, it was clear to everyone else that it wasn't a dog at all, but a lamb. I kid you not!

This might sound laughable and I

have no wish to insult anyone's intelligence, but con artists are very convincing. The lady with the lamb fell foul of her own self importance, I believe, because she had paid thousands for this 'dog' and she obviously knew nothing whatever about canines, or any other animal for that matter.

# LIVER CAKE

Liver cake is a very simple recipe - even I can make it, and I never make cakes for the human inhabitants of the house!

300g liver
300g self raising flour
2 eggs
1 clove garlic (or tablespoon ground garlic)
water / milk

Put the liver and flour plus garlic in a blender, whizz until like a thick paste. Put the eggs in a jug, add same volume of milk or water (I use water). Add the egg mixture to the blender and whizz some more until smooth. Pour into baking tins, bake 30-45 mins at about 180 centigrade.

Turn out of tins, divide into portions (makes about 8-10 good sized portions) and freeze until needed.

**Warning**: if your blender starts to struggle, you will find that bits of tissue from the liver are wrapped around the blades...remove these and carry on!

**Further Warning**

Before it is actually cooked, liver cake stinks! Choose a day when you can open all your windows!

**<u>All temperatures are centigrade</u>**

Dogs love liver cake. I've never met a dog who didn't so if you want to train your dog, tempt him with liver cake.

# POEMS

A kind person sent me this poem when I lost my Joshua, who was only three. I hope it speaks the truth - I hope he is waiting at Heaven's gate.

## <u>MY GRANDEST PUP</u>

(author unknown)

I'll lend you for a little while
My grandest pup, He said.
For you to love while he's alive
And mourn for when he's dead.
It may be one or twenty years,
Or days or months , you see.
But, will you, till I take him back,
Take care of him for me?
He'll bring his charms to gladden you,
And should his stay be brief,
You'll have treasured memories
As solace for your grief.
I cannot promise he will stay,
Since all from earth return.

But, there are lessons taught on earth
I want this pup to learn.
I've looked the wide world over
In my search for teachers true.
And from the throngs that crowd life's
lanes,
With trust, I have selected you.
Now will you give him your total love?
Nor think the labor vain,
Nor hate Me when I come
To take him back again?
I know you'll give him tenderness
And love will bloom each day.
And for the happiness you've known!
Forever grateful stay.
But should I come and call for him
Much sooner than you'd planned
You'll brave the bitter grief that comes
And someday you'll understand.
For though I'll call him home to Me
This promise to you I do make,
For all the love and care you gave
He'll wait for you, inside Heaven's Gate.


Lord   Byron   wrote **Epitaph   to   a**

**Dog** which is inscribed on Boatswain's tomb. Boatswain was a Newfoundland and the poet risked his own life by nursing him through his last days, suffering from rabies.

Although Boatswain was a gentle giant, the poem can apply to any dog.

When some proud Son of Man returns to Earth,
Unknown by Glory, but upheld by Birth,
The sculptor's art exhausts the pomp of woe,
And storied urns record who rests below.
When all is done, upon the Tomb is seen,
Not what he was, but what he should have been.
But the poor Dog, in life the firmest friend,
The first to welcome, foremost to defend,
Whose honest heart is still his Master's own,
Who labours, fights, lives, breathes for him alone,
Unhonoured falls, unnoticed all his worth,

Denied in heaven the Soul he held on
earth -
While man, vain insect! hopes to be
forgiven,
And claims himself a sole exclusive
heaven.
Oh man! thou feeble tenant of an hour,
Debased by slavery, or corrupt by power
-
Who knows thee well must quit thee with
disgust,
Degraded mass of animated dust!
Thy love is lust, thy friendship all a cheat,
Thy tongue hypocrisy, thy heart deceit!
By nature vile, ennobled but by name,
Each kindred brute might bid thee blush
for shame.
Ye, who perchance behold this simple
urn,
Pass on - it honours none you wish to
mourn.
To mark a friend's remains these stones
arise;
I never knew but one - and here he lies.

    In his Will, executed in 1811, Byron

instructs that he be buried in the vault with Boatswain. In fact the dog's tomb at Newstead Abbey, is bigger than Byron's own.

# EPILOGUE

This book is primarily about the Cavalier King Charles Spaniel and J-Lo in particular. She is a very popular dog and has a huge facebook following, but the main reason for this book is to raise funds for her ever increasing veterinary expenses.

She is due for yet another operation soon, this time on her brain. With unexpected recoveries from so many problems and illnesses, she is certainly a little miracle dog. I'm sure that most humans, finding themselves with so many ailments, would not keep smiling as she does.

Thank you for reading.

### THE END

Thank you for reading about J-Lo and her mission. To become a friend of J-Lo go to

http://www.jlosmission.co.uk/
membership-join/

If you want to donate, please
visit J-Lo's Go Fund Me page here
https://www.gofundme.com/to-
help-jlo

J-Lo would like to remind all
potential dog owners that her breed
is not the only one which can suffer
from this debilitating and
heartbreaking disease. No matter
what breed you decide on, whether
it be a tiny companion or a huge
working breed, make sure you visit
the appropriate breed club and find
out all you can.

A fully health tested puppy will
cost you more money, but not as
much as the veterinary expenses
and heartache you will pay later by
not doing your homework.

J-Lo wishes all dogs a long and
carefree life and a human as
devoted as her own.